D0883534

MAR 0 8

The Library of
NATIVE AMERICANS

The Karankawa
of Texas

Greg Roza

The Rosen Publishing Group's
PowerKids Press™
New York

For Abigail

Special thanks to Dr. Mariah Wade, professor of Anthropology at the University of Texas at Austin. Special thanks also to the Texas Archaeological Research Laboratory.

Published in 2005 by The Rosen Publishing Group, Inc.
29 East 21st Street, New York, NY 10010

Photo and Illustration Credits: Cover (41AS1- 80), title page, pp. 3, 6 (41CL3- 63-31), 12, 17, 22, 52 (41VT1-1512/7-1-737), back cover, Matthew Peeples, Texas Archaeological Research Laboratory, The University of Texas at Austin; p. 4, Mindy Liu; p. 9, The Thomas Gilcrease Institute of American History and Art, Tulsa, Oklahoma; p. 10, Betty Pat. Gatliff, SKULLpture® Lab; p. 14, Artwork by Frank Weir, painted for Texas Shores magazine, Texas Sea Grant College Program, 1992. Reprinted with permission of the publishers; p. 18, Private Collection/The Stapleton Collection/ Bridgeman Art Library; p. 19, Courtesy of Hunt Institute for Botanical Documentation, Carnegie Mellon University, Pittsburgh, PA; p. 21, Catalogue No. 5458, Department of Anthropology, Smithsonian Institution; photo by D.E. Hurlbert; pp. 25 (41SP43-C25), 28 (41NU11-C49) Texas Archaeological Research Laboratory, The University of Texas at Austin; pp. 31, 51 Courtesy of Texas State Library and Archives Commission; pp. 33 (Manuscript 4275), 35 (Manuscript 502a-b) National Anthropological Archives, Smithsonian Institution; p. 36, Jim Glass; pp. 40, 45 © Bettman/Corbis; p. 43 © National Portrait Gallery, Smithsonian Institution/Art Resource, NY; p. 47, Library of Congress, Geography and Map Division; p. 48–49 Courtesy of Mission Espiritu Santo, Goliad State Park, Texas Parks and Wildlife Department, photos by Dallas Hoppestad; pp. 54-55, © George H. H. Huey/Corbis

Book Design: Erica Clendening
Book Layout, Karankawa Art, and Production: Mindy Liu
Contributing Editor: Shira Laskin

Library of Congress Cataloging-in-Publication Data

Roza, Greg.
 The Karankawa of Texas / by Greg Roza.— 1st ed.
 p. cm. — (The library of Native Americans)
 Includes index.
 Summary: Discusses the origins, social structure, spiritual beliefs, and daily life of the Karankawa, with an emphasis on who they were and why the tribe is now extinct.
 ISBN 1-4042-2870-5 (lib. bdg.)
 1. Karankawa Indians—History—Juvenile literature. 2. Karankawa Indians—Government relations—Juvenile literature. 3. Karankawa Indians—Social life and customs—Juvenile literature. [1. Karankawa Indians. 2. Indians of North America Texas.] I. Title. II. Series.

 E99.K26R69 2005
 976.4'1004979—dc22

 2003022205

Manufactured in the United States of America

Contents

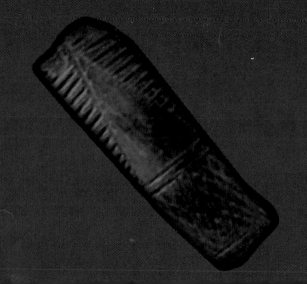

Where the Karankawa Lived

Galveston Bay

Galveston

Karankawa

Gulf
of
Mexico

Matagorda Bay

Nueces River

Corpus Christi Bay

Corpus Christi

Texas

Mexico

Gulf
of
Mexico

One

Introducing the Karankawa

The Karankawa Indians included five groups of Native Americans who shared a common culture and a common language. These tribes lived on the gulf coast of Texas, roughly between Galveston Bay and Corpus Christi Bay. The five tribes were the Cocos, Cujanes, Coapites, Copanes, and the Carancaguases, from which the name Karankawa came. Although historians are not sure what the name Karankawa means, many think that it may mean "dog-lovers" or "dog-raisers." We know that the Karankawa were not insulted by this name because they would use it to refer to them-selves. There is evidence that other Native Americans called them "wrestlers," "barefoot," and "people who walk in the water."

The Karankawa were a migratory people. This means that they moved to different places in search of food throughout the course of the year. Migration was an essential part of the Karankawa's sur-vival. If their food supply was low because of a change in season, the tribe had to find a new place with enough food for them to eat. The Karankawa spent the fall and winter in large groups on the coast of Texas or on the barrier islands just off the coast of Texas. During the spring and summer months, the Karankawa broke up into smaller groups and moved inland.

This map (left) shows the area along the Texas coast where the Karankawa lived.

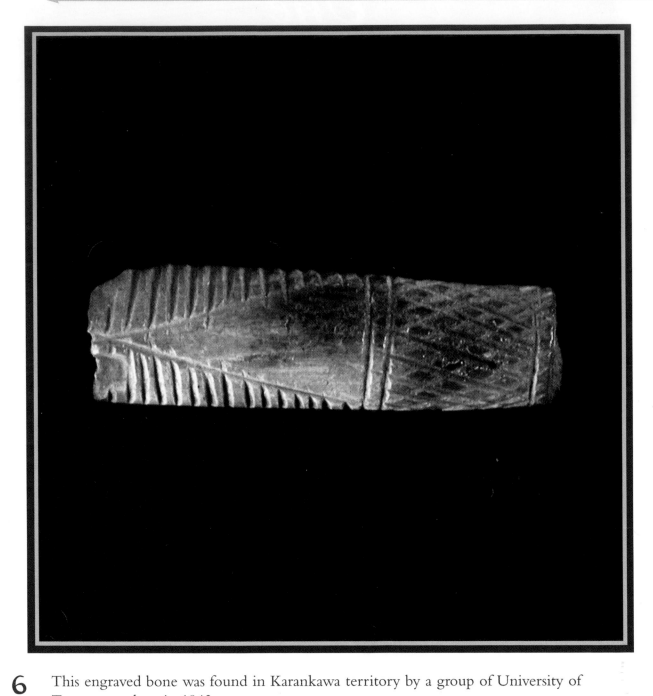

6   This engraved bone was found in Karankawa territory by a group of University of
Texas researchers in 1943.

Compared to other Native American groups, not much is known about the Karankawa Indians. This is because they left very few objects behind for us to study to learn about their culture. Since they moved so often, the Karankawa kept very few personal possessions. It was difficult for them to carry things from one camp to another several times a year. Archaeologists, scientists who study the past by digging up and carefully examining old buildings and objects, have studied the Karankawa. They found simple tools, pottery, and remains of food the Karankawa had eaten, but discovered little else.

The Origin of the Karankawa

Most scholars believe that sometime between 40,000 and 13,000 years ago, people from Asia came to North America by crossing a frozen land bridge that stretched from Siberia to Alaska. During that time, the climate was much colder than it is now. Glaciers, or great sheets of ice, covered much of North America. These people, ancestors of the Native Americans, slowly moved south. By 12,000 years ago, some of them had reached the tip of South America. Little is known about these very first Americans. During the thousands of years that followed, these groups spread out, populating different regions of the Americas. No one knows for sure when the first Karankawa lived in Texas. Scientists have uncovered evidence to suggest that the tribe was there as early as 2500 B.C.

Understanding the Karankawa

Of all the Native American groups in Texas—and perhaps the whole United States—the Karankawa are one of the most misunderstood tribes. Most of what we know about the Karankawa has come from European explorers who encountered the tribe in the 1600s and 1700s, and from Mexicans and Americans who began to populate Texas in the early 1800s. These people often regarded the Karankawa as a violent, warlike tribe. Confrontation between natives and white people was common. This was often the result of European aggression. Many explorers and settlers of Texas showed the Karankawa little or no respect. They were interested in obtaining land and they felt that the Karankawa were in their way. A fundamental element of Karankawa culture was to take action against those who did not treat them fairly. It is possible that this aggression was in defense of their culture and their tribe. Therefore, the Karankawa's reputation as a confrontational people may not be entirely true—or, at least, may reveal only one side of the story.

Sadly, the Karankawa culture is extinct. As Europeans populated North America, many native cultures were wiped out. Some Karankawa left Texas. Some of them joined other tribes or converted to Christianity. Many others were killed by white settlers in the area. The story of the Karankawa has become a jigsaw puzzle that ethnologists, scientists who study cultures, and archaeologists have struggled to put together since the death of the culture.

8

Carancahueses

This undated watercolor by Lino Sánchez y Tapia shows two Karankawa Indians fishing on the Texas coast. The painting is labeled *Carancahueses*, a slightly different spelling of Carancaguases, one of the five tribes that made up the Karankawa.

9

Two
Karankawa Technology

The Karankawa led simple lives dedicated to basic survival. They spent their time fishing, hunting, gathering plants, protecting themselves from the environment and from their enemies, and constructing the tools they needed in order to live. They worked when they needed to and rested when they could.

There were times when it was difficult for the Karankawa to find food. They had to migrate and adapt to the cycles of nature in order to survive. The Karankawa knew the lagoons, bays, islands, and rivers of the coast very well. They were also familiar with the inland forests and prairies, as well as with other groups of Native Americans with whom they shared hunting grounds. This familiarity helped them find what they needed to survive. It also allowed the Karankawa to avoid confrontation with Europeans for many years, since early Europeans had difficulty mapping and navigating the coastal area.

Appearance and Clothing

The Karankawa men were tall and muscular. There are some reports that call the men giants, but others say their average height

This sculpture of a Karankawa woman was created by Betty Pat. Gatliff in October 1988. Gatliff is a forensic sculptor, an artist who studies human remains and other scientific evidence to create sculptures of people who are no longer alive.

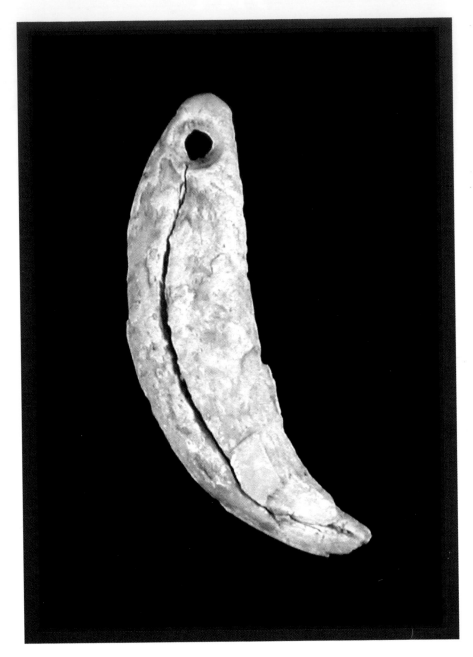

12 This tooth from an unidentified animal has a hole drilled in it. It was probably worn around the neck as a pendant. The tooth was found on the shores of Oso Bay in Texas.

was around 6 feet. The women were typically shorter. Both men and women had long, thick black hair. Men often wore their hair in braids, but women generally did not.

Karankawa clothing was simple. When it was warm outdoors, the Karankawa wore very little clothing or none at all. Men wore loincloths that the women made from deerskins. Women wore knee-length deerskin skirts. Most children did not wear clothing in warm weather. In the winter months, the Karankawa sometimes wrapped a deer or bear hide over their shoulders. Generally, neither men nor women wore anything on their feet or heads.

Ornamentation

Karankawa women rarely adorned themselves. Men, however, wore tight necklaces made of shells and seeds, and rings they got from white settlers. Men also wove bright strips of cloth and rattlesnake tails into their braided hair. They often pierced one nipple, sometimes both, with a long reed or branch. Men and women wore a plain bracelet made of deerskin on their left wrists.

Karankawa men and women used tattoos to decorate their bodies. Each member of the Karankawa tribe had the same blue pattern painted on his or her face. There was a curved line or circle on each cheek, a line at the corner of both eyes, two lines at the corners of the mouth, and three vertical lines on the chin. They sometimes painted shapes and figures on their skin with red and black paint as well.

14 This watercolor, called *The Karankawa Indians of the Texas Gulf Coast*, was painted in the 1990s by Dr. Frank A. Weir. The painting was featured in *Texas Shores* magazine with an article discussing the Native Americans who once inhabited the Texas coast.

The Karankawa considered a flattened head to be a sign of beauty. To achieve this look, infants in Karankawa society went through a process of head flattening. Soon after a child was born, his or her mother would place a board on the child's forehead and secure it with a piece of animal hide. Traditionally, the board stayed on the infant's head for a year, a day, and a night. The board kept the child's skull from developing naturally, flattening it above the eyes.

The Karankawa people often covered their bodies with shark oil to keep mosquitoes and other insects from biting them. Shark oil also kept their skin soft. The oil's very strong, offensive smell sometimes helped keep Europeans from getting close to the Karankawa, too.

Shelter

The Karankawa lived in simple huts made of sharpened willow poles and animal skins. The huts had to be easy to take down and put back together because the Karankawa moved so often. It took about twelve 15- to 18-foot (4.5- to 5.5-m) willow poles that were about an inch (2.54 cm) thick to make a one or two-family hut. When a group reached a new camp, the women worked the sharpened ends of the poles into the ground in a circle about 10 to 12 feet (3 to 3.6 m) in diameter. The poles were placed about a yard (0.9 m) apart. The women then bent the poles over so they met in the middle and tied the ends together with strips of deerskin. They hung larger pieces of deerskin and buffalo skin over the poles for shelter. The animal skins protected the Karankawa from the wind and Sun. However they provided no shelter from the rain.

After the women had constructed the huts, the men would start fires inside for warmth and cooking. Each man had a set of supplies for starting the fires. This set included a flat piece of wood with parts cut out, a long, rounded stick, and dried leaves and twigs. To start a fire, a man would spin the rounded stick against the wood he held between his hands. Eventually, the friction from this process would result in heat and a thin trail of smoke. The man then quickly placed the dried leaves and twigs over the smoking stick. He then blew on the smoking pile until his breath helped the leaves and twigs catch fire. Karankawa families usually kept their fires burning all the time. They sat and slept around the fires on deer and bison hides.

Food

The Karankawa were not farmers. They were hunters and gatherers, and depended on their environment's natural resources for survival. The tribe moved around during the year as the seasons affected their food supply.

During the fall months, many kinds of sea animals were abundant along the gulf coast of Texas and the barrier islands. The barrier islands are located between the ocean and the mainland coast. The position of these islands enables them to protect the coast from the crashing ocean waves. As a result of this, the

The Karankawa were very talented fishermen. They used bows and arrows with arrowheads, such as these, to catch their fish.

lagoons and bays of the mainland have calm and sandy bottoms—a perfect environment for shellfish to breed. The Karankawa ate large quantities of shellfish, such as oysters, scallops, quahogs, and other clams. Redfish, trout, catfish, tuna, and turtles were also part of their diet.

The Karankawa were skilled at fishing. They used a simple bow and arrow as their fishing tool. To catch a fish, a man stood in shallow water with an arrow drawn, waiting for a fish to swim near. He would almost always hit his mark. Europeans who witnessed this type of fishing were amazed by the Karankawa's ability to hit targets moving underwater.

The Karankawa were also experienced hunters and gatherers. During the warmer parts of the year, they moved inland where they hunted for deer and bison on the Texas plains. To make hunting easier, they would burn all but a few grassy areas near their camp. This allowed the Karankawa to lure bison and deer to the remaining grazing areas, making it easier to hunt. While they mainly hunted bison and deer, the Karankawa also hunted ducks and other birds, bears, panthers, and a fox-like dog that lived on the Texas prairie. They also ate different types of bird eggs.

18 Shellfish and fish, such as the trout pictured above, were an important part of the Karankawa diet when they lived on the coast during the colder parts of the year.

M. E. Eaton del.

Flowering joints of *Opuntia lindheimeri*.
1. Orange-flowered race. 2. Red-flowered race.

Prickly pears, the small, sweet fruit of the prickly pear cactus, were among the many wild fruits and vegetables the Karankawa ate.

Plants were an important part of the Karankawa diet, too. Depending on the season and the tribe's location, the Karankawa had access to many different types of plants, such as cattails, roots, berries, wild grapes, prickly pears, and persimmons. They ate nuts, including acorns, pecans, and seeds. As white settlers began to populate the area, the Karankawa added new foods into their diet. This included cattle meat, flour, and coffee.

Most of the Karankawa food was simple and required little preparation. Many of their meals were eaten raw. When they cooked their food, they either roasted it in the ashes of their fires, or boiled it in traditional ceramic pots or metal kettles they acquired from white settlers. They sometimes made a bread-like food from crushed acorns, crushed roots, and ash. Most of the time, they ate their food with their hands, even though evidence suggests that they had roughly carved spoons.

Crafts, Tools, and Weapons

The Karankawa did not have many tools. They did not need them to perform most of their daily activities. Those tools that they did make were very simple. Men used stones and shells to make simple knives, scrapers, hammers, awls, and adzes. Women used flat, round stones to grind seeds and fruit. They also carved simple spoons out of wood, made pins and needles from fish bones, and made thread from deer sinew, or muscle tissue. They used the pins, needles, and thread to

The Karankawa mostly used bows and arrows while fighting. However, in some cases, they used other weapons, such as this war club.

make simple blankets and mats to sleep on, as well as to make the few articles of clothing they wore.

The Karankawa made clay pots with rounded bottoms for storing and cooking their food. They used a coiling technique to make their pottery. This means that they rolled out the clay into long, narrow strips. They then wound the strips into the shape of a container and smoothed out the sides. Some of the pots were plain while others were painted with asphaltum, a natural tar-like substance that washes up on the gulf coast of Texas. This black substance was used to paint decorative designs and figures on the pots. The Karankawa also used asphaltum as a glue to seal containers.

Very little is known about the arts and crafts of the Karankawa because they left almost nothing behind. We know they had knives made from stones and shells for preparing food. There is evidence that some Karankawa shaped conch shells into decorative patterns, and used other shells to make beads and pendants. They also made several basic musical instruments. They filled gourds with stones to make rattles and hollowed out pieces of wood that were then scraped with a stick to make a droning sound. Some Karankawa also made wicker baskets, but this was not a common practice.

Bows and arrows were among the few weapons used by the Karankawa. The bows were very tall—almost as tall as the people—with strings made of tightly twisted deer sinew. After the arrival of European settlers, the Karankawa used other weapons and tools, such as knives and axes.

The Karankawa made different pots and containers for cooking and storing their food. This artifact (left) is believed to be a bottleneck from Karankawa pottery. It was discovered near Corpus Christi Bay.

Digging Up the Past

Much of our information about the Karankawa comes from evidence that scientists have uncovered in Texas. These scientists, called archaeologists, dig up soil to see what people from earlier times have left behind. A location that has been studied by archaeologists is called a site.

Native groups often left behind broken parts of tools or craftwork as well as bones from the animals they hunted. These clues to the past are known as artifacts. They help experts understand what life was like for the Karankawa many years ago.

There are two main groups of sites that archaeologists have found to be old Karankawa camps. The first group is made up of sites along the Texas plains and prairies, where the Karankawa spent each spring and summer. The second group of sites is found along the Texas shoreline, where the Karankawa lived during the fall and winter.

One important site, known as the McKenzie Site, is located on the plains of Texas near the mouth of the Nueces River. Archaeologists uncovered pieces of stone tools, knives, and arrowheads. They also found 196 pieces of pottery at the site, which experts believe represent nine separate pots. While most Texas natives did not make pottery, evidence shows that the Karankawa did.

Archaeologists uncovered different animal bones at the site, including deer and bison. The bones were scattered in a semi-circle around a group of fire pits, which were most likely where the Karankawa had cooked their food. Artifacts found at locations such as the McKenzie Site have helped experts determine that the Karankawa lived on the Texas prairies during the spring and summer months.

Archaeologists dig up land to find evidence left by people who lived many years ago. These archaeologists are working at a site near Corpus Christi Bay in June 1967.

Another important source of information about the Karankawa is the evidence found at the Holmes Site. This site is at the edge of Corpus Christi Bay, a body of water that leads to the Gulf of Mexico. Archaeologists found a great number of artifacts at the Holmes Site that suggested the Karankawa had lived there for many years.

While digging at the Holmes Site, scientists found parts of knives used to open clams, as well as other tools. They uncovered more than 2,400 pieces of pottery and 18 pieces of pipes. The scientists also found small blocks of asphaltum.

A large amount of small fish and shellfish bones were found at the Holmes Site. This evidence helped archaeologists determine that the Karankawa lived in the coastal areas of Texas during the fall and winter. Fish and shellfish were most plentiful in the area during the cooler months of the year.

The artifacts found at the McKenzie Site and the Holmes Site have given experts clues to figure out the Karankawa's past. The many bones and tools found at the Holmes Site, as well as other coastal sites, have helped us to determine that the Karankawa lived on the coast, eating fish and shellfish when it was plentiful. The artifacts found at the McKenzie Site, and other sites on the Texas prairie, suggest that the Karankawa moved to these areas as the changing weather lowered the supply of fish on the coast.

Traveling

The Karankawa moved often and brought very little with them to a new campsite. They generally stayed at a camp for an entire season. If the food supply was low, however, they often broke into smaller groups who were easier to feed. They kept very few personal possessions. They only carried with them what they would need to set up camp in a new location. This included their shelters, clothing and hides, bows and arrows, a few simple tools, and some pottery.

Since they lived so close to the water, the Karankawa used wooden canoes called dugouts to travel from one place to another. The Karankawa made these canoes by flattening one side of a large log. They would then taper, or narrow, the ends of the log so the dugout would move smoothly through the water. The Karankawa left the bark on and hollowed a place to sit in the center of the dugout.

The dugouts were not stable enough for travel on the open sea, but were perfect for short trips through the shallow waters of the Texas coast. Women and children sat in the center while the men used long poles to guide the dugout through the waters near the shore. After Europeans arrived in North America, the Karankawa also used skiffs, which are flat-bottom row boats, to travel from one camp to another. After the Spanish settlers arrived in the area, the Karankawa were introduced to horses as a means of transportation. They were not known as good riders, however, and preferred to walk on land or to travel by water.

Three

Other Features of Karankawa Life

The Karankawa Indians were made up of five tribes who shared cultural traditions. Food supply determined the size of the groups in which they lived. Places where food was plentiful became important social gathering points. Groups of Karankawa would meet in these places to exchange information, find mates, and work together to collect food. The tribes sometimes joined and traveled together to increase their chances of survival.

Social Structure

The Karankawa had four main levels of social organization. The smallest group was known as a band. A band had about 50 or 60 members who were generally of the same family line. During the spring and summer, when the Karankawa had to migrate inland for food, they broke up into these bands.

Groups of bands who lived together are known as macrobands, which means total band. Macrobands were made up of about 400 to 500 people and were found along the Texas coast during the fall and winter, when shellfish was plentiful. These larger groups were loosely organized and had no single leader. Macrobands served an

We know where the Karankawa lived because they left evidence behind. The deer bones pictured at left were found near other evidence of Karankawa life at a site on the coast of Texas.

important function for the Karankawa. As bands gathered together, they were able to share information, perform rituals, and strengthen ties across Karankawa society as a whole.

Groups of macrobands, the third level of social organization, made up each of the five tribes of the Karankawa Indians. These tribes, the Cocos, Carancaguases, Cujanes, Coapites, and Copanes, ranged in size from 400 to 1,600 people. The fourth level of social organization is the Karankawa tribe as a whole. This title includes all five tribes because they shared a similar language, a similar system of survival skills, and similar seasonal migration patterns.

Government

There is no record of the Karankawa having an organized government. Unlike other Native American tribes, the Karankawa had no chiefs. Within each band, however, were two important men that each performed a special service for that group. The first man acted as the speaker for the band. He advised the group on worldly matters. The second man was the group's spiritual leader, who was called a shaman. While very little is known about the religion of the Karankawa, we do know that shamans were a very important part of their culture. Shamans were usually older men. The Karankawa believed that shamans had special powers and could cure people of sickness. In Karankawa tradition, a person cured by a shaman would give the shaman all of his or her possessions, and perhaps the possessions of his or her relatives as well.

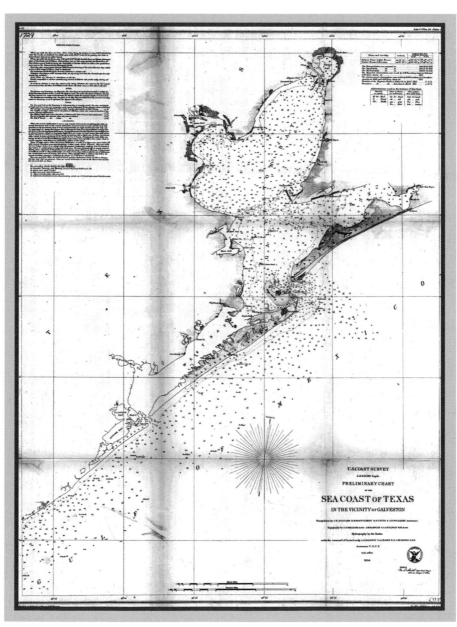

This 1856 map shows the Galveston region of the Texas coast. Evidence suggests that the Karankawa spent time in this area.

Communication

The tribes who made up the Karankawa Indians all spoke the same language. Each group had their own dialect, but everyone was able to understand one another. The Karankawa had two ways to converse with other tribes or bands over distances. They used high-pitched whistles to signal to each other over short distances. For longer distances, they used smoke signals. On a clear, windless day, the Karankawa could create more than 20 different signals with a column of smoke that burned from a fire in a small pit.

Roles of Men, Women, and Children

Young men were considered very important in Karankawa society. They were often referred to as warriors and spent much of their time in battle. Men were also responsible for hunting and sometimes gathering food. Their other chores included tending fires, making and decorating pottery, and making weapons.

Women did most of the work for their tribe. They made the shelters, gathered wood, water, and food, and prepared the food for their groups. Women were not considered equal to men, and were not always treated with respect. They did, however, fulfill important roles in Karankawa society. As warriors, men were forbidden from crossing the boundaries that separated Karankawa land from the lands of

In 1916, John Swanton Reed, an American scientist who studied cultures, published *Two New Vocabularies from Texas Tribes*. The book discusses several Native American languages, including the different Karankawa dialects.

other native peoples. A man's presence on another tribe's land could be considered a threat to that tribe. Women could cross these lines without causing a problem and could trade with other people for materials the Karankawa needed. During wartime, women sometimes crossed these lines to plead with the conflicting tribes for peace. It is believed that women were not respected, yet they had an essential role in Karankawa life.

Older members of Karankawa society served as the tribe's memory, telling stories and passing on legends. For the most part, however, the elderly were not respected. The Karankawa felt that the older tribe members were wasting food that should have been given to children, the future of the tribe, instead.

Karankawa children were treated with great affection, especially by their mothers. They had no responsibilities and were rarely punished. The Karankawa considered children their greatest assets because they would continue the existence of the tribe.

Religion

We know very little about the Karankawa religion or spiritual beliefs. Scientists have not uncovered any records of legends or creation myths. We do know that the Karankawa held ceremonies and had celebrations involving music, singing, and dance. This evidence has been provided by several white settlers who witnessed these rituals. None of these settlers understood the rituals'

Ceremonies
(Contin'd from 17.)

raising himself to an erect posture). The chant rose and fell in a melancholy cadence and occasionally all the Indians joined in swelling the chorus, which associated in the exclamations:

hā-ā héya hé-i, héya, hâya ke

and ended in an abrupt hai! very loud and far-reaching. They had three instruments of music to accompany the chant : 1) one a large gourd filled with calculi or shot (a stiff rolled up) frequently shaken (a deer skin was under it for resonance); 2) a fluted notched piece of wood held upon the knees, over which a stick was quickly drawn making a droning noise (like drones = bees) 3) the third was a sort of rude flute softly blown in measure (or in time) with the chant ; no airs were played upon it)

This ceremony, called fandango by the whites (absurdly enough!) was continued throughout the night and as time went on, became louder and more weird in the chants. The fire was made to burn furiously and had a frightfully lurid effect

Above are Alice Oliver's notes on Karankawa ceremonies, collected by Albert Samuel Gatschet in December 1888. In these notes, Oliver described the musical instruments used during a particular ceremony. They included a hollowed-out gourd filled with small objects that produced a rattling sound, as well as several flutes.

36 The yaupon tree is a small evergreen holly native to the southeastern United States. The Karankawa used the leaves from this tree to make a tea.

significance, however, and the Karankawa offered no explanations of their customs.

We know of one ceremony that was described in the writings of a young white girl from Texas named Alice Oliver. When Oliver was a child in the 1830s, her father owned a ranch near a Karankawa camp. She spent quite a bit of time with the tribe, witnessing their everyday life and even learning their language. Shortly before Oliver died, she revealed everything she knew about the Karankawa. Her writings reveal that the tribe members welcomed her into their lives.

Oliver wrote about a particular Karankawa ceremony she saw, which she called the "solemn festival." This festival took place during a full moon or after a successful hunting trip. Oliver claimed the men gathered in a tent and silently prepared a strong, bitter tea made from the leaves of the yaupon tree. The tea was passed around in a ceramic, or clay, bowl from which each man drank in total silence. As this occurred, a man dressed in animal hides chanted and danced around the others. After a while, the others joined in the dancing and chanting, and some men played musical instruments. The celebration often lasted through the night and became what Oliver called "loud and weird."

Other Karankawa rituals have been described with much less detail. Some involved smoking tobacco. Others included whistling or watching the setting Sun. Unfortunately, very little is known about these ceremonies.

Marriage

Marriage was common in Karankawa society, but it appears that it was not considered an important union. Reports by European settlers stated that married couples were somewhat indifferent to each other. Marriages often did not last, unless the couple had a child. Shamans generally had two or three wives.

In Karankawa tradition, when a man and woman married, the man gave everything he had caught while hunting to his wife's parents. The wife's parents, in return, would do the same for their new son-in-law. The Karankawa thought it was bad luck for the wife's relatives to talk to, or even look at, her husband. It is unclear, however, how long the husband and his in-laws practiced this custom.

Death Traditions

The Karankawa wept every day for a year when a person died. Children were especially missed, and the weeping was particularly sorrowful. Old people usually received no special treatment in Karankawa society when they died. Most people were buried in the spot on which they passed away. While traveling, Karankawa men often left ill members of the group behind to die alone.

The Karankawa had a special custom following the death of a shaman. Shamans were not buried. They were cremated during a high-spirited ceremony involving dancing. The shaman's bones were ground into a powder. Members of the shaman's family would then blend his ashes with water and drink the mixture. Each year, the family would celebrate the anniversary of the shaman's death by scarring themselves. They made small cuts in their skin in tribute to the person who died.

Gift Giving

Hospitality was extremely important to the Karankawa way of life. Gift giving was an especially meaningful tradition. Often, small groups or even whole bands would give everything they had to a visiting group. In proper tradition, the visiting group gave their hosts something in return. Both hosts and visitors expected the tradition. If it was not followed, it could be seen as a serious offense in the eyes of a Karankawa.

Weeping

Another Karankawa tradition involved weeping. When two men met each other after a long period of time apart, they would sit and weep together for half an hour. The Karankawa believed in removing all feelings of grief or sadness between host and visitor as quickly as possible. After the weeping ended, the host offered all of his possessions to the visitor. In some cases, the Karankawa even extended these rituals to Europeans who were exploring the Texas coast.

Four

Encounters with Europeans

Most of what we know about the Karankawa comes from reports made by European explorers who observed and even lived with the tribe. Reports by Mexicans and American colonists who began to populate Texas in the early 1800s also add to our knowledge. Some of the European reports do not offer specific information about the Karankawa, but are more general memories about all of the natives living on the Texas coast at that time. We can safely assume that all of these groups, including the Karankawa, shared some or all of the characteristics mentioned, based on later reports by Mexican and American colonists.

Cabeza de Vaca

The earliest recorded contact between Europeans and the Karankawa took place in the fall of 1528. A few months earlier, a Spanish expedition of 600 men led by an explorer named Pánfilo Narváez landed in the area that is today known as Florida. The treasurer for this group, a man named Álvar Núñez Cabeza de Vaca, would become the first European to live with the Karankawa. His writings about the time he spent with

In 1537, Cabeza de Vaca returned to Spain to publish his writings about his experiences with the Karankawa. He lived in Spain until his death in 1557. This piece of art (left), featuring Cabeza de Vaca, was done in 1880.

the Karankawa are some of the earliest we have regarding any Native Americans.

Narváez and his men met many hardships as they traveled from Spain to the gulf coast of Texas. In fact, two-thirds of the men died at sea. Many others were separated from the crew during violent storms. In November 1528, a group of about 80 of these men that had been separated, led by Cabeza de Vaca, reached Galveston Island on the southeastern shore of Texas. The men were starving, exhausted, and scared of what they might encounter in this new land. Cabeza de Vaca sent one of the stronger men out to investigate the area. The man returned shortly with a water jar, a dog, and some fish that he had found in a nearby village. Following him were more than 100 native warriors. Fearing the natives, Cabeza de Vaca quickly offered them beads and small metal bells as symbols of peace. The natives took the gifts and offered Cabeza de Vaca arrows, a sign of friendship. The natives then left, but returned the next day with food for the weakened Spaniards.

Almost all of the Spaniards died in the following months. Only four of them, including Cabeza de Vaca, survived. These four men spent about four years living with the Karankawa. The Karankawa were sometimes very friendly to the Spanish explorers. Other times, the Karankawa treated the men like slaves, even killing some of them. Cabeza de Vaca was taken as a slave. Believing that he had special powers, the Karankawa wanted Cabeza de Vaca to serve their village. After some time, they persuaded him to act as both a shaman and a trader for their village. Cabeza de Vaca learned their ways and used this knowledge to his advantage. His reputation grew among other native groups of the Texas coast and he was respected as a powerful man. He treated the Karankawa and other native groups he met with respect. Cabeza de Vaca's writings about the time he spent with the Karankawa are an extremely important source of information about the tribe.

Henri Joutel

For more than a century, there was little or no contact between Europeans and the Karankawa. In 1685, a French explorer named Rene Robert Cavelier Sieur de La Salle led an expedition to Texas. The purpose of the

La Salle's expedition to Texas in 1685 marked the first contact between Europeans and the Karankawa in over 100 years. This pen-and-ink portrait of La Salle was done by artist Jacques Reich.

mission was to establish a permanent French presence in Texas. La Salle and his men built Fort St. Louis near Matagorda Bay on the southeastern coast. La Salle's most trusted lieutenant was a man named Henri Joutel. La Salle often left Joutel in charge of the fort while he explored different parts of Texas.

Joutel made many observations about the Karankawa and other native people who lived in the area. He recorded a great deal about the Karankawa's appearance and everyday life. However, Joutel observed the tribe from a distance. He did not get close enough to them to offer information about their religious beliefs, rituals, or customs. Joutel was not involved in their society.

From Joutel's writings, we know that La Salle was assassinated by a group of his own men while visiting other Native American groups in eastern Texas in 1687. Joutel and his crew traveled north. Those settlers left at Fort St. Louis were later killed by the Karankawa. No one knows for sure why the Karankawa attacked Fort St. Louis. However, Joutel's writings suggest that the act of war was one of revenge for the Karankawa, for an offense committed against them.

Spanish Missions

Over the next 100 years, many French and Spanish explorers came to the land known today as Texas. In the 1690s, the Spanish began establishing a string of missions in eastern Texas. These missions

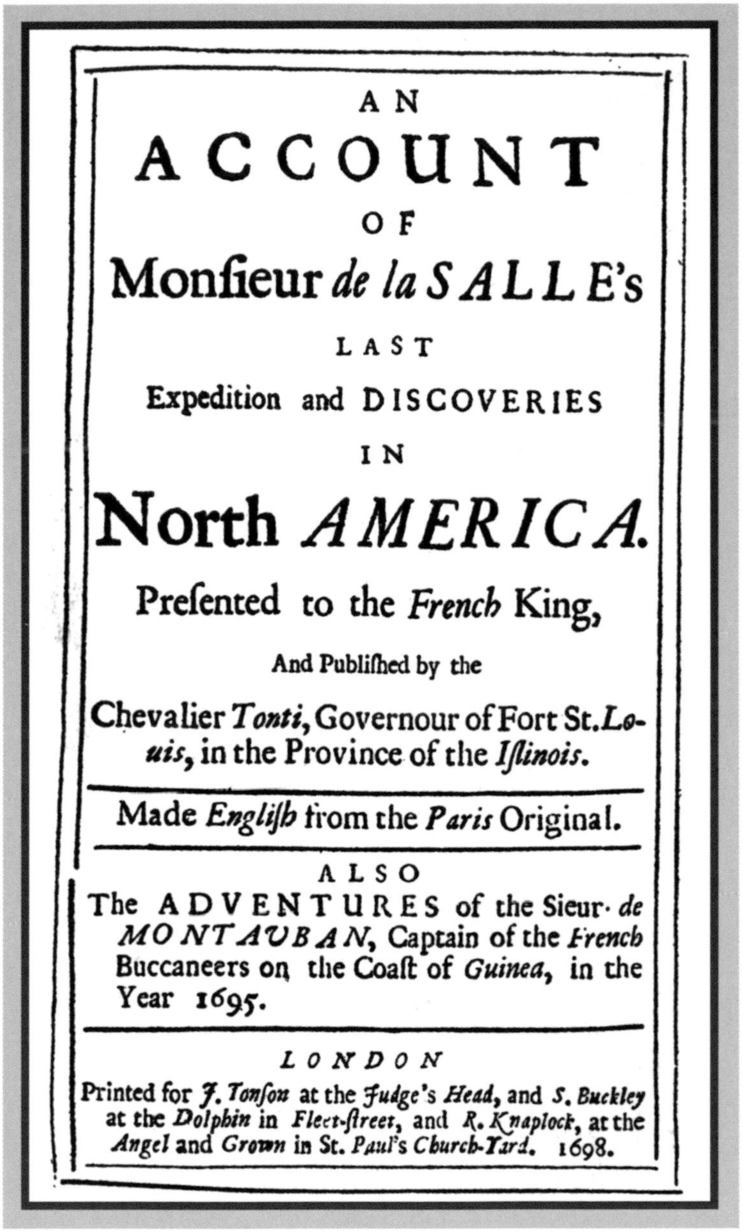

AN
ACCOUNT
OF
Monſieur *de la* SALLE's
LAST
Expedition and DISCOVERIES
IN
North AMERICA.
Preſented to the *French* King,

And Publiſhed by the

Chevalier *Tonti*, Governour of Fort St. *Louis*, in the Province of the *Iſlinois*.

Made *Engliſh* from the *Paris* Original.

ALSO
The ADVENTURES of the Sieur· *de MONTAUBAN*, Captain of the *French* Buccaneers on the Coaſt of *Guinea*, in the Year 1695.

LONDON
Printed for *J. Tonſon* at the *Judge's Head*, and *S. Buckley* at the *Dolphin* in *Fleet-ſtreet*, and *R. Knaplock*, at the *Angel* and *Crown* in St. *Paul's Church-Yard*. 1698.

In 1698, Chevalier Henri de Tonti, La Salle's lieutenant, published the journal pictured above. It is considered one of the most reliable accounts of La Salle's last expedition. This journal describes La Salle's attempt to establish a colony in Texas as well as his murder. In 1714, Henri Joutel published his own account of what happened.

45

were settlements in which the Spanish would forcefully persuade local native tribes to convert to Christianity and adopt Spanish culture. The missions were created to help secure the northern border of New Spain against the French. New Spain, the territory ruled by the Spanish, stretched from Florida to northern California. The Spanish hoped to overcome the natives and establish a permanent hold on the Texas coast.

The Karankawa resisted the Spanish attempts to convert them to Christianity and force them to adopt Spanish culture. The first attempt was at the mission Espíritu Santo de la Bahia. The mission was built in 1722 near Matagorda Bay. Spanish soldiers attempted to lure the Karankawa to the mission by promising them a feast. Once the Karankawa arrived, however, Spanish soldiers attacked them. A battle took place, leaving many Karankawa warriors and one Spanish leader dead. The mission was abandoned and rebuilt further inland.

More Spanish missions were built across Texas. Some native groups of inland Texas eventually left behind their own beliefs for the Spanish way of life. The missions offered them food and shelter, which was tempting to people living off of the land. The Karankawa, however, remained uninterested in converting to Spanish culture.

When treated kindly by the Spanish settlers, the Karankawa often responded with kindness. When treated aggressively, however, they responded with aggression. The Karankawa cleverly took the food and shelter offered by the missions only when the

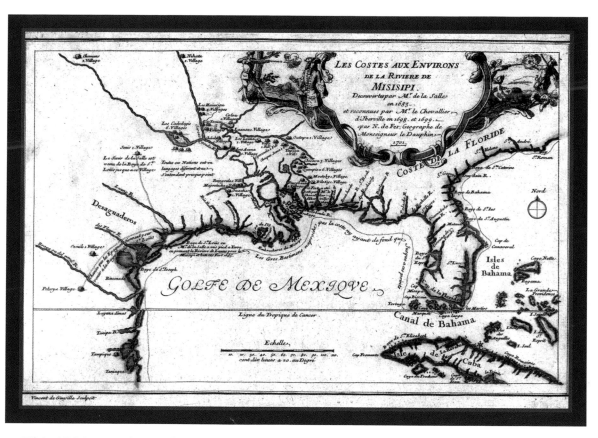

This 1701 map shows the location of several Native American villages La Salle encountered while exploring the coastal areas of the southern United States. Some of these areas are believed to be Karankawa villages.

changing seasons left them with no other choice. When natural sources of food became more abundant, however, the Karankawa quickly left the missions.

By the end of the eighteenth century, Spanish influence in the area was very strong. There were more than 20 missions across Texas. Many Karankawa went to live in the Spanish missions. Some Karankawa even converted to Christianity.

The mission Espíritu Santo de la Bahia was first established in 1722 by the Spanish. It has since moved twice, and now stands on the San Antonio River near Goliad. In 1848, the building was used as a college. In 1931, it became recognized as a state park.

Mexican and American Colonists

By the early nineteenth century, American colonists were building more and more communities across North America. In 1820, an American from Connecticut named Moses Austin wanted to establish an American colony in Texas. The Spanish government was in control of Texas at the time, and Austin had to ask for their permission to do so. The Spanish agreed. Moses Austin died shortly after this, leaving his son, Stephen Austin, to carry out the plan. Stephen Austin successfully brought more than 5,000 American settlers into the heart of Karankawa territory over a period of 10 years.

By the 1830s, many Mexicans had settled in Texas as well. There was tension between the American colonists and the Mexican settlers over who should control the land. The Karankawa were caught in the middle of this dispute. There were frequent confrontations between the Karankawa and the growing number of American colonists and Mexican settlers. Unlike the Spanish missionaries, the colonists were not interested in converting the Karankawa to their way of life. They wanted to acquire fertile Texas land and natural resources. They felt the Karankawa were in their way and did not hesitate to kill them—or any natives—they encountered. Both the Mexican settlers and American colonists felt that Texas was *their* land—and that no one should stand in their way as they took over the area.

Stephen Austin is remembered for settling and developing Texas. This portrait was created in New Orleans by an unknown artist shortly before Austin's death in 1836.

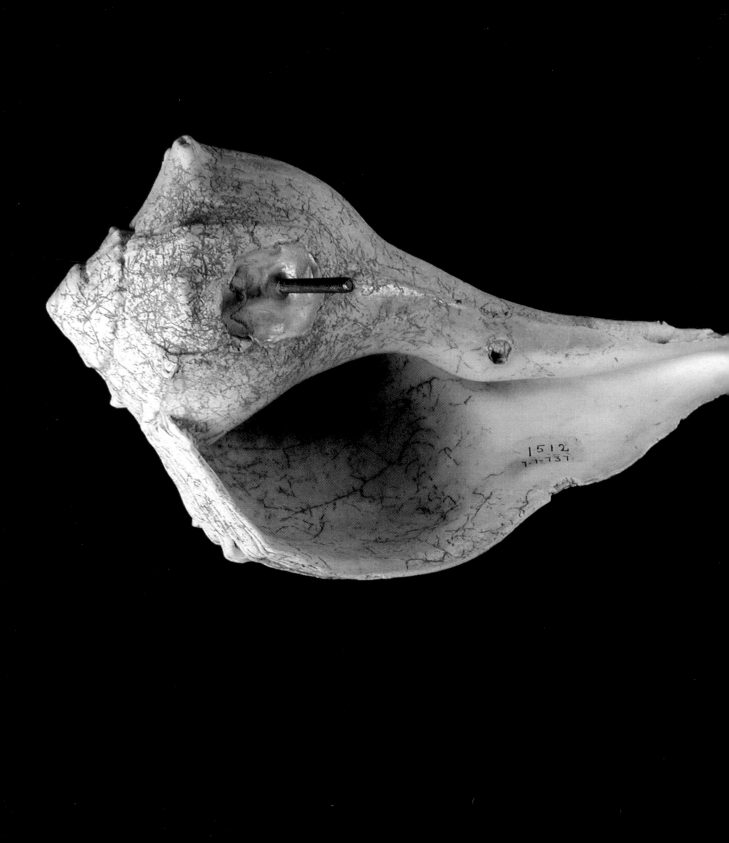

Five

What Happened to the Karankawa?

When Texas became an independent republic in 1836, the Karankawa population had already been greatly reduced. By the 1840s, there were only scattered groups of the tribe along the Texas coast. Many of them moved south to Mexico to escape pressure from the growing population of Texas settlers. Once the Karankawa arrived in Mexico, however, the Mexican government accused them of attacking locals. The tribe was quickly pushed back into Texas.

By the middle of the nineteenth century, the Karankawa were no longer the proud, self-sufficient people they had once been. Some of them were assimilated into white society by the missions they had resisted for years. In 1858, a small band of Karankawa was attacked and killed by a Texas force who was determined to end the tribe's existence. No one can say for sure that this band was the last of the Karankawa tribe. After this attack, however, the Karankawa were considered extinct. Some of them may have escaped back into Mexico. Others may have joined different native tribes.

This conch shell (left) was found in Karankawa territory during the 1930s. The importance of the hole, emphasized by a metal object, is not known.

The Karankawa survived 300 years of European invasion, Mexican and American colonization, and attempts to wipe out their culture. In the end, they were forced to accept their fate as a

dying culture. As more people attempt to piece together the history of this tribe, perhaps we will gain more insight into the Karankawa civilization.

While the Karankawa Indians are considered extinct, they are not forgotten. The Karankawa civilization is an important part of the history of North America.

Timeline

13,000 to 40,000 years ago	Ancient ancestors of the Native Americans travel from Asia to North America.
Around 2500 B.C.	Scientific evidence suggests this is the earliest presence of the Karankawa tribe on the gulf coast of Texas.
1528	A group of Spanish explorers led by Álvar Núñez Cabeza de Vaca are the first to make contact with the native tribes of coastal Texas, including the Karankawa. Cabeza de Vaca is taken as a Karankawa slave and lives with the tribe for about four years. His reports about the tribe later become one of the most important sources of information about the Karankawa.
1685	French explorer Rene Robert Cavelier Sieur de La Salle leads an expedition to build Fort St. Louis near Matagorda Bay. Henri Joutel, La Salle's trusted lieutenant, observes the Karankawa and documents their habits. The Karankawa attack the fort, killing all but a few Frenchmen.

1690s	The Spanish begin to establish a string of missions in Texas to convert native peoples to Christianity and to secure the borders of New Spain against the French.
1722	The mission Espíritu Santo de la Bahia is built in the heart of Karankawa territory. It is abandoned soon after and rebuilt further inland.
1820	Moses Austin receives permission from the Spanish government to establish an American colony in Texas. Over the following 10 years, his son, Stephen Austin, successfully brings more than 5,000 settlers into Karankawa territory.
1830s	Alice Oliver spends time with the Karankawa, documenting their everyday lives and learning their language. Her writings later become a key source of information about the tribe.
Late 1830s	Tension rises between American colonists and Mexican settlers living in Texas. Both groups feel the Karankawa stand in the way of them taking over Texas.
1836	Texas becomes an independent republic.

1840s	Only scattered groups of the Karankawa exist along the Texas coast. Some of them attempt to move south to Mexico, but are pushed back into Texas by the Mexican government. Some Karankawa convert to Christianity, while others join remaining native tribes.
1858	A small band of Karankawa is attacked and killed by a Texas force hoping to wipe out the tribe.
Late 1850s	The Karankawa disappear as an identifiable cultural group.

Glossary

adapt (uh-DAPT) To change because you are in a new situation.

adorned (uh-DORND) Decorated.

adzes (AD-zez) Axe like cutting tools used to shape wood.

artifacts (ART-uh-fakts) Objects made or changed by human beings, especially tools or weapons used in the past.

asphaltum (AS-fawlt-um) A tar-like substance that washes up on the Texas shore on the Gulf of Mexico, among other places.

assets (ASS-ets) Things or people that are helpful or useful.

assimilated (UH-sim-uh-layted) Absorbed, or blended into, the cultural tradition of a group of people.

awls (AWLZ) Sharp metal tools for making holes in leather or wood.

barrier islands (BA-ree-ur EYE-luhndz) Long, sandy islands that run parallel to a coastline.

cattle (KAT-uhl) Cows, bulls, and steer that are raised for food or for their hides.

colonists (KOL-uh-nists) People who live in a newly settled area.

cremated (KREE-ma-tuhd) Burned to ashes after death.

droning (DRO-ning) Deep murmuring, humming, or buzzing.

dugouts (DUHG-outs) Canoes made by hollowing out a tree trunk.

extinct (ek-STINGKT) No longer existing; to have died out.

friction (FRIK-shuhn) Rubbing that causes heat.

hide (HIDE) An animal's skin.

indifferent (in-DIF-uhr-uhnt) Not interested in something or someone.

migrate (MYE-grate) To move from one place to settle in another.

missions (MISH-uhnz) Groups of people sent to a foreign land by a religious organization to spread its faith to foreign people, and the buildings housing those groups.

pendants (PEN-dants) Hanging ornaments, especially those worn on necklaces.

persimmons (pur-SIM-uhnz) Orange-red fruits that are shaped like plums and are sweet and soft when ripe.

prickly pears (PRIK-lee PAIRZ) Small, sweet fruit of the prickly pear cactus.

quahogs (KWAW-hawgz) Round, edible clams that have thick, heavy shells.

sinew (SIN-yoo) Animal tendon.

skiffs (SKIFS) Wide, flat rafts made by tying multiple narrow logs together that can be propelled through shallow water by poles or sails.

spiritual (SPIR-uh-choo-uhl) To do with religion.

Resources

BOOKS

Bedichek, Roy. *Karankaway Country*. Austin, TX: University of Texas Press, 1974.

Favata, Martin A., and José B. Fernández (trans.). *The Account: Álvar Núñez Cabeza de Vaca's Relación*. Houston, TX: Arte Público Press, 1993.

Foster, William C. (ed.), Johanna S. Warren (trans.). *La Salle Expedition to Texas: The Journal of Henri Joutel, 1684–1687*. Austin, TX: Texas State Historical Association, 1998.

Gatschet, A. S. *The Karankawa Indians, the Coast People of Texas*. Cambridge, MA: Periodicals Service Co., 1991.

Newcomb, W., Jr. *The Indians of Texas: From Prehistoric to Modern Times*. Austin, TX: University of Texas Press, 1972.

Ricklis, Robert A. *The Karankawa Indians of Texas: An Ecological Study of Cultural Tradition and Change*. Austin, TX: University of Texas Press, 1996.

WEB SITES

Due to the changing nature of Internet links, PowerKids Press has developed an online list of Web sites related to the subject of this book. This site is updated regularly. Please use this link to access the site:

http://www.powerkidslinks.com/lna/karanka

Index